BEDWORTH
IN OLD PHOTOGRAPHS

MARKET PLACE, C. 1913. Detail from a postcard by H.R. Lovett.

BEDWORTH
IN OLD PHOTOGRAPHS

COLLECTED BY
JOHN BURTON

ALAN SUTTON

Alan Sutton Publishing Limited
Phoenix Mill · Far Thrupp · Stroud · Gloucestershire

First published 1988
Reprinted 1992

British Library Cataloguing in Publication Data

Burton, John
Bedworth in old photographs.
1. Warwickshire. Bedworth, history
I. Title
942.4'83
ISBN 0-86299-550-7

Front Cover Illustration: South side of Market Place c.1913.

For my long-suffering family

Typesetting and origination by
Alan Sutton Publishing Limited.
Printed in Great Britain by
WBC Print Limited.

CONTENTS

I HAVE JUST ARRIVED AT BEDWORTH

COMIC POSTCARD, overprinted with the name of the railway town. One can imagine the comments this figure would provoke as he walked up King Street from the station.

INTRODUCTION

It is a truism to say that everything changes, but in Bedworth it really does. The Bedworth of the early 1960s would have been easily recognisable to a resident returning after 50 years. Buildings were altered but essentially Bedworth's centre remained the same shape, in the same buildings, over those tumultuous 50 years. However, anyone leaving in 1960 and returning in the late 1980s would be staggered by the changes. Thirty years later only a handful of the earlier buildings remain.

Regeneration is not new. Though the Bedworth of 1960 had examples of older buildings, it was largely created in Victorian times and reflected the prosperity (such as it was in what had always been a significantly poor community) of the weaving and mining industries. There was, from the Victorian developers, a uniformity of building style, brick-pattern and roof-shape which spoke as strongly of speedy Victorian regeneration as our tall residential blocks do today, as they reflect the urgent cynicism of the 1960s or the go-getting entrepreneurs of the 1980s in their dockland warehouse redevelopments. Architecture is an eloquent historian, and the humblest building tells a story.

Seven or eight publications about Bedworth have appeared over the years, but they have been written histories rather than pictorial ones. In 1980 Alan Robinson and Mort Birch broke new ground with their collection of photographs, *Bedworth As It Was*, which opened the eyes of many to what the town used to be like.

In this book the pictures show old Bedworth street by street in a sequence of 260, starting in the Market Place (now All Saints Square) and radiating clockwise round the town. I have tried to keep photographic records since the late 1960s. For views of the town before then I have relied on help from earlier enthusiasts. In recent years I have shown slides about Bedworth and many photographs have joined the collection as a result of the kindness of people attending those talks. Since 1981 The Bedworth Society has encouraged, not to say indulged, my interest.

The presence of pre-1900 photographs is largely a matter of luck in a town like Bedworth. Perhaps a chemist with time and enthusiasm recorded his town, but luck is needed for his prints, or plates, to have survived. After 1902 we benefit from the huge numbers of postcards produced to satisfy collectors from all social classes, whose enthusiasm continued unabated until the First World War. Even this Edwardian golden age was subject to commercial pressures. There were many postcard manufacturers, mostly based in London. The biggest, like Tuck and Valentine, produced cards all over the country. However, there was a critical size of town below which large companies were uninterested. Nuneaton, with its George Eliot links and its size, attracted major firms like Stengel, and Steward & Woolf. Bedworth did not. Consequently we rely for early pictures on the work of local photographers, printers, stationers and post offices.

Bedworth should be grateful to Messrs Oates, Mole, Lovett and Parsons for their first-class postcards. A Midlands company, Teesee, sold excellent cards all over North Warwickshire throughout the 1920s. At least three sets featured Bedworth. During the next thirty years, little was produced until the 1960s. We rely during this fallow period on the chance records of enthusiasts. Among these were the Edmands brothers, from the Tower House in High Street. They took thousands of photographs, especially of cars and trains; sixteen of their pictures are in this book. During the 1950s and 1960s some pictures of an amazing quality were taken by Ken Bosworth. I reproduce seven of them with a humble sense of admiration for his skill.

This book concentrates on Bedworth itself. It includes a section on Collycroft, but stops at the Bottom River, so Griff is excluded. To the east it does not reach Marston Jabbett or Coalpit Fields. Little Bayton and Exhall are also omitted. The book could have been twice the size just in covering its existing area. Perhaps the publishers will be encouraged to commission a second volume which can include the outlying areas. I am always interested to see pictures and there are still gaps in my collection. For instance, I have seen no good pictures of Church Street, the old Congreve Way and most of the yards in Bedworth. If this book uncovers some new pictures it will have been worthwhile. The local paper, museum and library can all provide my address.

A full list of acknowledgements is at the end of the book. I have to emphasise my gratitude to all the photographers whose work is featured. Using other people's photographs is rather like plagiarism, yet a book of this nature is impossible without them. I comfort myself with the thought that by recording the Bedworth I have known over the last twenty years, and for who knows how many more to come, I shall be supplementing the work of those earlier photographers and promoting a sense of continuity. I am happy to present my meagre efforts to future enthusiasts so that the process of recording what we have been, and what we have seen, can continue.

The Nicholas Chamberlaine Almshouses and the Market Place

BEDWORTH ALMSHOUSES. Though not photographs, these are interesting as possibly the earliest representations, other than maps, of Bedworth. The Nicholas Chamberlaine Almshouses were rebuilt on their present site in 1840, at a cost of £8,500. The pictures show the scale of the buildings. They must have seemed enormous to a village or township of some 4,200 inhabitants.

QUADRANGLE, BEDWORTH ALMSHOUSES. The two prints were produced by Day and Haghe, lithographers to Queen Victoria, and presented to the Governors by the architect, Thomas Larkins Walker, in 1839. Copies were sold to raise money for the construction of a school house on Bedworth Heath. In 1988 The Bedworth Society sold a limited edition reprint to help restore the Pumphouse at the Almshouses.

TRANQUIL SCENE AT THE ALMSHOUSES, 1911. Residents had to be Bedworth-born church-goers, and on formal occasions and for church had to wear uniform. The bee hive-like building in the centre is the ivy-covered Pumphouse, where residents drew water before the water tower provided an improved piped service. Sweet peas were growing up the stakes surrounding the tree. They were planted by the lodge-keeper and warden, Mr Randle.

ROYAL VISIT TO BEDWORTH. On 10 July 1934 the Prince of Wales visited the Almshouses and planted an oak tree. It still thrives. The line of buildings which formed a yard between J.C. Smiths and the Maypole shops had three storeys and followed the line of modern Congreve Walk. To the left are council officials; William Johnson jun. is on the left of the Prince of Wales. Next to him, wearing the chain of office, is Councillor Edward Tyler. Between them, but a pace behind, is Dr Lionel Orton and the man with his hand to his face is headmaster Alfred Lawrence.

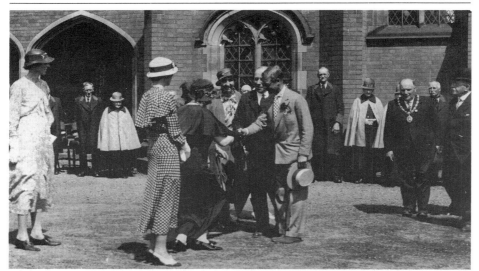

ROYAL VISIT, 10 July 1934. The Prince of Wales being introduced to local dignitaries in front of the Governors' Hall. Some residents (originally called inmates) are lined up behind in their official coats and capes.

BUN DAY, Bedworth Almshouses. It is a long-standing tradition that during Whit week, when the Governors have their meeting, all the pupils from the church schools in town are presented with a bun. In this picture two of the boys are Fred Orton on the right and Tommy Neal on the left. Mrs Fitzroy Newdegate is presenting the buns. Among the men are William Johnson jun., Jack Johnson, J.F. Dewis, A.H. Lawrence and Mr Cope. It dates from the mid-thirties.

GOVERNORS' HALL, Bedworth Almshouses. Male residents posing for the camera at a celebration in the hall of the Almshouses. The holly leaves suggest it is Christmas, as do the hats. The hall is modelled on Elizabethan design, with wood panelling and a balcony. The coat of arms belonged to former trustees.

FEMALE RESIDENTS at the same party. It appears that the meal is over.

FOUR GENERATIONS OF RANDLES. Seated at the front are Mr and Mrs Randle senior, with their four great grandchildren. Their son and daughter-in-law are standing behind them in the middle of the back row. Their grandson, Thomas Henry Randle, is on the back left, and his wife is on the back right. The four great grandchildren are Harry, Horace and Frank, with baby Vera Randle (now Sephton) at the front. They are the children of Mr and Mrs Thomas Henry Randle.

CORNER OF MARKET STREET AND KING STREET. Market Street was a short section of road which ran into Market Place. All the buildings shown here have disappeared during the early 1970s. The roof-line of the Almshouse Lodge is on the left. That was demolished first and is now a flower-bed next to Boots. The slightly Flemish-look at roof-level was on a number of buildings. The post-box was outside the old Midland Bank, in use for a while as the Post Office.

BARCLAYS BANK stood where Boots now stands. Barclays added the stone cladding for impression. Originally a sub-office, the branch opened full time under manager Reg Wilson on the day the General Strike started in 1926. There is an alley in the middle of the picture.

WALKING DOWN THE ALLEY shown on page 15 revealed this rural setting. Originally it was the slaughterhouse for the butcher next to the bank. Most of these shops had enclosed gardens and fruit-trees behind them, despite being in the centre of town.

EAST SIDE OF MARKET STREET, where Boots and W.H. Smith now stand. On the left is Parsons & Sherwin, formerly Linney & Horobin (in the town since 1830). Next was Skeltons, formerly Oates (see page 18), and to the right, boarded up, the Oxfam shop had been Boots, and long before that it was Topp's.

ESSENTIAL SHOPS like ironmongers have lost their distinctiveness of earlier years. Linney's supplied basic necessities for over a century. They were stalwarts of the community, and the Linney Memorial Prize is presented still to a hard-working Bedworth pupil.

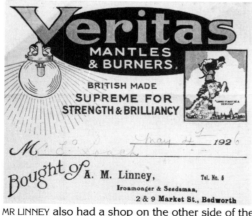

MR LINNEY also had a shop on the other side of the road by 1926. The Veritas advertisement shows how slow electricity was in coming to Bedworth. By 1939, Parsons, Sherwin, with branches in Nuneaton and Hinckley, had taken over. They ran the shop until they closed for redevelopment c.1970.

INTERIOR OF OATES THE CHEMIST. This marvellous picture came from a plate taken by Mr Oates in 1900 or 1901. Amongst the items on the shelves are teething rings, numerous cough drops in a variety of flavours, cyclists' lozenges, gravy salt, carbolic acid, extract of malt, glycerine and cucumber, smokers' tooth powder, and numerous proprietary medicines.

ADVERTISEMENT FOR NEURALGIA MIXTURE from the same year as the shop above. One shilling a bottle was a lot of money at a time when a man would earn perhaps one pound a week. At that time, one shilling would have bought a gallon of ale, but that might not have cured the neuralgia.

MARKET STREET FROM THE CHURCH C.1970. This view was only possible when the shops and Lloyds Bank were demolished on the west side of Market Street and High Street. The passage between the two blocks came out in King Street. With redevelopment the curve in the street disappeared to make a rectangular All Saints Square.

BEDWORTH'S ANSWER TO ROMAN MOSAICS. In the doorstep of his shop (above, left) Mr Oates had the family name picked out in mosaic tiles. Marriage changed the name to Skelton, and the firm is now in Congreve Walk.

WATSON'S THREE PRIZE SOAPS

WATSONS MATCHLESS CLEANSER

WATSONS MATCHLESS CLEANSER · WATSONS MATCHLESS CLEANSER

GUARANTEED FULL WEIGHT, AS STATED ON WRAPPERS, WHEN MANUFACTURED.

EVERY WRAPPER A COUPON · WATSONS BIG PRIZE SCHEME

A PERFECT DISINFECTANT

NUBOLIC SOAP

LAUNDRY.

THE HOUSEHOLD FAVOURITES
FOR CLEANLINESS & HEALTH.

INVOICE FROM ALFRED TOPP, 24 October 1914. Mr Topp ran the shop which is shown at the top of page 19 before it became Boots. In 1914 many Bedworth men were in mining or industrial work and no doubt Watson's prize soaps were applied vigorously. You can feel the Nubolic soap doing you good.

STOP! HAVE YOU GOT
A. Y. Z.

If so, you will not fail to recognise that

ALBERT GARDNER,

MARKET PLACE, is the Leading Clothier and Outfitter in BEDWORTH.

. . . .

GARDNER for Clothing you cannot excel.
GARDNER for Cheapest of prices as well.
GARDNER for everything quite up-to-date.
GARDNER for Value, permit me to state.
GARDNER of Bedworth in Memory Treasure.
GARDNER for Suits of the Finest to Measure.
GARDNER for Juveniles Clothing A 1.
GARDNER I'll warrant is beaten by none.
GARDNER solicits from each one a call.
GARDNER will give satisfaction to all.

ADVERTISEMENT FOR ALBERT GARDNER, 1901. A far cry from today's slick, professional advertising copy. It has a rugged charm. Bedworth seems to like doggerel; it is still printed in the local paper.

MARKET STREET, 1913. One of the finest postcards produced; a detail is on the cover. The Almshouse Lodge is on the extreme left. The Bull and the Newdegate Arms were next to each other. Church Street goes off to the right, behind the girls. All the buildings have gone now, to reveal the parish church which stands across the south end of the square.

STANDARD VIEW OF MARKET PLACE, taken during the 1920s, probably from an upper room in the Newdegate Arms. The building on the extreme left was run by Enoch Edmands. Jeannie Broadbent worked there as a young woman and has very vivid memories of it.

THE MAYPOLE, which opened here some time just before the First World War, was a much frequented shop in the centre of town. Beyond it is J.C. Smiths store. Later, the Maypole moved to the other side of Smiths. This side of the shop is Edmands. The building remained, but the next photographs show how it changed.

MARKET PLACE, late 1920s. Edmands' shop is now occupied by George Mason, offering strong competition to the Maypole. The yard at the side is the one seen in the distance on page 11. After the Maypole moved, the site was used by The Candy Store, and at the side of it was Bend's fresh fish shop.

ONE OF BUNNEY'S SHOPS. By this time (mid-1960s) the Maypole shop had been demolished and the redevelopment had begun to the left of this shop, which is the same building that Enoch Edmands occupied before the First World War.

WORTHINGTON'S AND BUNNEY'S in Market Street, Collins in High Street, in the mid-1960s, before demolition. The line was pushed right back to where the Midland and Barclays banks now stand.

CONGREVE HOUSE, CHURCH STREET. Church Street ran between the pubs and Bunney's shop, and curved round to come out by the west door of the church. This house was owned by the very popular and much-loved Dr Lionel Orton, who moved away from the town when his house was purchased for redevelopment.

MARKET PLACE 1907. The picture shows the posts and chain which stood in front of the Almshouses. Above ground-floor level, the buildings on the left remained the same until demolition c.1970. The man in the foreground was Mr Alcott. He had just taken his granddaughter, aged five, to Hob Lane School and was on his way back to the pub he kept, the Cottage Tavern, in High Street (page 110).

J.C. SMITHS STORE c.1930. Smiths came to Bedworth from Stratford in 1901. Later they opened a branch in Nuneaton and eventually they were taken over by Debenham's. In Bedworth they gradually took over the adjacent shops. The youngsters seen watching the royal visit on page 11 are standing on the flat roof extension clearly visible in this picture.

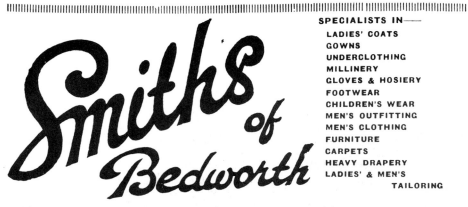

PARISH MAGAZINE 1936. There is a long tradition of offering value for money in Bedworth. Smiths took their advertising claims seriously. Long before this advertisement, Arthur Stevens began his working life at Smiths. As a very young employee he was given the tram fare to Coventry on his half-day and then had to walk back up the Foleshill Road, comparing prices. Next day Smiths would undercut them all. The other names in the advertisement are well remembered and some are still in business.

MARKET PLACE c.1911. The girls in the foreground are wearing typical clothing for the time which might well have been purchased at Smiths. In the middle is the shop belonging to Mr D.B. Mole. He sold newspapers, books and toys. Some wooden horses on wheels can be seen outside the shop. He also published some of the earliest postcard views of Bedworth.

WEST SIDE OF MARKET PLACE, 1930s. Most views of the Market Place are taken from the other (south) end, for the practical reason that from this end (north) the photographer would be looking into the sun, and after midday the shops were in shadow. Along the side of the white shop (Hursts) was White Lion Yard.

MARKET PLACE AND MILL STREET, mid-1960s. The White Swan block is still there, as is Harry's. The snack bar is now a flower-bed.

MARKET PLACE,

Bedworth, _____ 19/

And at NUNEATON

M _____

BOUGHT OF _____

GEORGE HURST & SON

Telegrams —"George Hurst, Bedworth."   Telephone No. 28

Wholesale & Retail Fruiterers & Confectioners.

AGENTS FOR ALL BEST MAKERS OF HIGH-CLASS CONFECTIONERY.

SHOPS SUPPLIED ON MOST LIBERAL TERMS.

BILL HEADING FROM GEORGE HURST, 1916. Hursts kept the shop shown at the top of page 28, next to Melias.

MARKET DAY, 1960s. When this photograph was taken the street market was coming to the end of its time and soon afterwards it was moved to its present site as redevelopment transformed the centre of town. The buses used to turn here and stop outside the Almshouses before setting off for Coventry.

OLD WHITE LION YARD, c.1950. There were many cottages in this yard and, when in the 1920s some of them were demolished, newspapers at the time called them the oldest in Bedworth. Others were taken over and used as workshops by J.C. Smiths. Also in the yard was the White Lion Inn, a building similar to the one here. This building was behind the pub and was bought by the Wesleyan Methodists to make way for their new chapel.

CORONATION PROCESSION, 1911. Taken from the Newdegate Arms, it shows how a town turned out for processions before the days of radio and television. The population of Bedworth in 1911 was 9,598 and most of them seem to be in the procession or watching it. Alterations are in progress to the shop occupied later by the Maypole Dairy.

PROCESSION INTO MARKET PLACE, 1950s. The men are wearing coats which suggests a cold day, possibly Remembrance Sunday.

WHIT WALK PROCESSION, 1920s. There is a church banner at the front, and Sunday School girls behind it. There are hanging baskets at the pub, rear left. Throughout the century the Market Place and Almshouses have provided a setting for countless processions and anniversaries.

Leicester Street to Marston Lane

LEICESTER STREET, 1970. The right of the picture shows the Hit or Miss pub, on the corner of Leicester Street and Chapel Street. The road was very narrow for the traffic it had to carry, especially before the bypass was built and Rye Piece Ringway constructed.

THE "HIT OR MISS" INN,

LEICESTER ST., BEDWORTH.

JACK RICHARDS - - **Proprietor.**

Eadie & Co.'s Fine Burton Ales & Stout,

On Draught and in Bottle.

Wines of the Best Quality.   Choice Cigars.

Considerable improvements have recently been effected at this House, which is now thoroughly up-to-date, and has every accommodation for Parties, Cyclists, &c.

ADVERTISEMENT FOR THE HIT OR MISS, 1907. It was a large and well-liked pub, much missed since demolition. No doubt the cyclists appreciated the improvements made on their behalf.

SHOPS IN LEICESTER STREET, 1970, just before demolition. The chequered brickwork is typical of mid-nineteenth-century buildings in this area. The Maurice Smart building was much older, almost certainly an eighteenth-century ribbon-weaving top shop. In the gable can be seen a bricked-up window; below that, on the second floor, were large north-facing windows, obviously built before the adjacent building which then effectively blocked out the light.

THE BUILDINGS ON PAGE 35 had gone when this was taken. It shows the narrow pavement and entrance to one of the yards which stretched back behind the street. To the left of the picture was Old Meeting Yard. The site is only now being redeveloped (1988).

LEICESTER STREET, 1970, before decimal coins, when cigarettes were 3s. 7d. for twenty. This imposing block was the last to go and held on just into the 1980s.

THE OLD MEETING CHURCH is Bedworth's oldest complete public building. Originally single-storey in 1726, the roof was raised in 1808. It is a superb example of an early nonconformist chapel and is now a listed building. The manse has gone, but the tree is still there. Hidden away from the main thoroughfare, it is an under-appreciated jewel.

ADVERTISEMENT FROM 1850. Thomas Adkins appears to have had a large stock. Presumably he managed to store the groceries away from the drapery.

MARK CLEVERLEY,
CLOTHIER AND PAWNBROKER,
Leicester-street, Bedworth.

MONEY LENT ON

PLATE, WATCHES,

Etc., Etc.

Temporary Loans to any Amount upon
all descriptions of Valuable Property
Confidentially Advanced.

Hours of Closing: Thursdays at 2, Saturdays at 11, other Evenings at 7 o'clock
AGENT FOR BRITISH EMPIRE MUTUAL LIFE ASSURANCE COMPANY.

PAWNBROKER'S ADVERTISEMENT, 1908. Mr Cleverley's shop was the front section, on to the corner of Leicester Street, of the bricked-up section of the building in the middle of the picture below. It is on the right-hand side of the block as shown on page 36.

MOST OF THE YARD has gone, but the front of Mr Moore's grocery shop was still open when this picture was taken. The spiky gable is on the Clear Hooters factory (Pickering's), the other side of Leicester Street.

IT WILL BE MANY YEARS before this open view is seen again. There was a brief time after demolition in Leicester Street when there was nothing from the Swan to Leicester Road. This is it!

THE BUILDINGS WENT GRADUALLY. This view in 1974 was only possible when the Hit or Miss was demolished to give an uninterrupted view of what is now Bede Arcade and Tesco.

LEICESTER STREET, 1975. Yards extended both sides of the central block, back to Sleath's Yard. Gordon Edwards moved from his shop here to the centre one shown at the bottom of page 36 in 1975. Five years later, demolition forced him to move again to Mill Street.

THE TINY COTTAGES, part of a much older Bedworth, were dwarfed by the buildings either side. Tesco now stands on this site. Before 1900 George Pickering bought the building and he and later his son ran the hat factory until 1953. In more recent memory it was occupied by Clear Hooters.

THE HATTERS' ARMS, 1976. Named from its proximity to Pickering's hat factory, whose chimney looms over it. In early days part of the building had been the telephone exchange (later in High Street). A narrow alley ran along the side of the cottages on the right. On page 42 is the yard the alley leads to.

ALLEYWAY TO SLEATH'S YARD, 1972. The wall on the right was the hat factory wall, presumably added after the houses and tenements on the left were built. They had the dubious privilege of windows facing north across a narrow passage to the factory wall. At the top was a side entrance to the factory and a row of houses running parallel to Leicester Street (see next picture).

SLEATH'S YARD, 1972. The passage in the previous picture came out by the car. This remaining section of Sleath's Yard was in a line with the road which still goes along the side of Harry's bakery.

TURNING HALF RIGHT from the picture at the top of this page and looking back towards Leicester Street, 1972. These derelict parts of the old yard backed on to the buildings on page 42. At the top centre is the gable of the factory. Moving further round to the right would bring us down by the side of Gordon Edwards' shop (page 40).

REAR OF HOUSES IN SLEATH'S YARD, 1972. These were the backs of the houses at the top of page 43. The picture was taken from the spot which is now the south-west corner of Tesco's, looking towards Leicester Street.

LEICESTER ROAD, BEDWORTH.

Aug 1 1916

Mr Pickering

Dr. to A. THORPE & SON,

Practical Farriers and General Smiths.

Horses Shod on the most
Scientific Principles.

Interest Charged on
Overdue Accounts.

All Kinds of Ironwork
made and Repaired.

Aug 2nd	*Paring Coll·*	*2 0*
2nd	*Repair Pump*	*1 0*

THORPE & SON were blacksmiths with premises near Pickering's factory, on what was then an unadopted road (now the Ringway), and some of their regular work came from attending the Pickering horses. The 1916 invoice, with its neat engraving, is a far cry from today's computerised accounting.

PICKERING SENIOR. George Henry Pickering (1857–1929) took over the hat factory in the late 1890s and extended and modernised it. Nevertheless, life was harsh for workers involved, especially in the stages involving chemicals which caused awful skin problems. Mr Pickering is wearing one of his own hats.

PICKERING JUNIOR. Samuel George Pickering (1896–1974) took over the factory in 1929 and had the misfortune to be running the business as hats became less popular. He is shown here being presented to Queen Mary in 1917 when he was 21. He had lost a leg in France and was lucky to survive the carnage; he owed his life to the bravery of a soldier who carried him to safety.

PICKERING'S HAT FACTORY, 1911. The boilers were made by Danks of Dudley. The boilerman was Tom Lydiatt from Old White Lion Yard. He kept the boiler in pristine condition and blew the factory hooter, audible all over town, at 5.30 and 5.50 a.m. The working day in 1911 was 6 a.m.–6 p.m.

DYEING AND FELTING PROCESS, 1911. The hoods (name given for the early stage of the hat) passed under a 100lb. oak hammer for the felting process while they were still wet. The machine, front left, was a hydro-extractor which dried the felts. The boys look very young. Among the workers were Phil Davis, Harry Barnet, Bill Beamish, Bill Shilton and T. Drakeford.

MACHINE TRIMMING ROOM, 1911. The very best quality hats went to the hand-trimming room; the rest were machine-trimmed here. Four of the girls in the picture were Florrie Richards, Annie Hazeldine, Rosa Holland and Edie Giles.

PROCESSION FROM LEICESTER ROAD. Tesco's main entrance is where the advertisements are. Mr Pickering lived at Ingleby, the double-fronted house second from the right. When this picture was taken the Mount Pleasant pub was being rebuilt. Later Mr Pickering senior built the house further up the road which later became the Rectory and is now to be a residential home for the elderly.

OLD AND NEW IN LEICESTER STREET, June 1981. The possibility existed for a few days of seeing the last old building disappearing on the left as Tesco was finishing its new store ready for opening – a startling juxtaposition.

LEICESTER ROAD, 1907. This view shows the houses, still there, at the corner of Leicester Road and the Ringway. Next was the Bear and Ragged Staff (now houses), then the Mount Pleasant and Pickering's house. This was one of few cards produced by a firm outside Bedworth. Ernest Ratledge from Rugby produced dozen of cards in the area. Sadly, most of them have faded badly, a reflection on poor darkroom technique.

THE BEAR AND RAGGED STAFF, c.1907. The building still exists as private housing. When the picture was taken the licensee was George Johnson. It appears to show him with his family outside the entrance.

LEICESTER ROAD, 1919. Travel 200 yards from the rebuilt town centre and the pre-First World War buildings are still there. It is unusual that every building on this card is still there, though the police station has been extensively changed.

STAFF AT LEICESTER ROAD SCHOOL, 1952. Back row: T. Griffiths, T. Colins, G. Brenchley, K. Harris, R. Morgan, G. White, B. Wyatt, G. Kirkbride. Seated: Mrs Boulstridge, R. Veasey, Miss Alexander, Mr Gray (Head), D. Robinson, H. Bailey, Mrs Rice, E. Sephton.

LEICESTER ROAD, c.1907. This row had only been built about ten years, as Bedworth stretched out towards Collycroft. It was an Ernest Ratledge postcard. The Rising Sun pub has changed; so has the Old House at Home (extreme right).

SECTION THREE

Collycroft

MARSTON LANE CORNER, c.1905. The children are on the spoil banks of Charity Colliery, all now hidden away under new housing. When this picture was taken the colliery was one of Collycroft's major employers. The Miners' Arms is still there.

PROCESSION OF NUNEATON DIXIELAND JAZZ BAND in the 1934 Carnival, passing the corner of Marston Lane.

THE MINERS' ARMS. A small girl pauses during sweeping-up operations for the picture to be taken. Externally the building has hardly changed at all.

THE MINERS' ARMS. This is an earlier view, taken when Herbert Bonsor was publican. Presumably the men are regular customers.

STALWART BEDWORTH WORKERS. An old and fading photograph showing two Bedworth miners (the one on the left carries a miner's lamp). Probably soon after the turn of the century. On the left is Herbert Bonsor (his wife is shown on page 55) who later took over as licensee of the Miners' Arms. The sticks show that these two were pit deputies.

ORCHARD STREET, COLLYCROFT, 1907. Unusually, the children are not spread out across the street as they were in so many contemporary street photographs. The cottages on the left have gone, but much else remains.

HIGHFIELD TERRACE, MARSTON LANE. This lovely informal group picture was taken c.1907. In the doorway on the left are the two Parsons girls. The two ladies are Mrs Fowkes and Mrs Bonsor. On the doorstep with her mother is Ida Fowkes. Leslie Bonsor is in front of her. The little girl with the hat is Florrie Fowkes. The houses were built in 1898 and are still there.

COLLYCROFT CHURCH SUNDAY SCHOOL. This dates from c.1912 and was no doubt taken before the start of a procession.

COLLYCROFT SUNDAY SCHOOL TEACHERS in 1912 or 1913. On the back row are Ernest Fowkes, Beattie Jacques, Priscilla Jacques, Agnes Brindley, Elsie Fowkes. Front row: Maggie Jacques, Alice Wheatley, May Knight and Gladys Orton.

COLLYCROFT SCHOOL, 1911. The school closed in the late 1960s and transferred to Henry Bellairs. Collycroft had a distinguished line of head teachers and many successful pupils. Two houses stand on the site now, although part of the wall on the left is still there.

COLLYCROFT EVENING SCHOOL, c.1902. Mr W.H. Alexander, at this time headmaster at Collycroft, re-instituted evening classes which ran successfully for adults and young people with a desire to improve their education. The picture was taken by C.H. Oates (see page 18).

CLASS IV AT COLLYCROFT, c.1905. The little girls with their hob-nailed boots are delightful. Mr Alexander was headmaster at Collycroft until 1907. He is on the right; his picture appears on countless photographs over a forty-year period when he was a considerable influence in the town.

CLASS I, COLLYCROFT INFANTS, perhaps thirty years later than the top picture; the children are much less formally dressed.

Lower Collycroft, Nr. Bedworth.

LOWER COLLYCROFT, 1907. Interesting that Collycroft was referred to as 'Near Bedworth'. This card was sold by Mr Harris who ran the sub-post office from the shop shown on the left. The building jutting onto the pavement is on page 64.

SCHOOL HOUSE, COLLYCROFT, c.1902. The head teacher's house which faced the main road, the school being behind it and facing Orchard Street. W.H. Alexander is seen standing outside the house with his wife Sarah, and young daughters Margaret and Elizabeth. The building is now a hotel.

COLLYCROFT COUPLE, c.1912. Thomas Daniel Hunt and his wife Emma outside their cottage in Warehouse Yard, at the side of the Cricketers.

COLLYCROFT CHILDREN in Warehouse Yard. There must be a lot of these youngsters still around to recall their childhood days in Collycroft.

COLLYCROFT COTTAGES, typical of early housing for miners or weavers. Some of the tiny front rooms were used as workshops or shops. Near to these houses was the cycle shop belonging to Mr Parker.

MRS DAY OUTSIDE HER SHOP in the early 1960s. Even since then some of the titles advertised here have disappeared.

COLLYCROFT FC 1913–14. Back row: W. Darlison, J. Orton, F. Tunnicliffe, E. Topp, Holt, T. Wright, J. Marsden, H. Kelly, C. Bonsor, B. Moore, F. Orton. Centre: B. Hood, J. Twigger, H. Hood. Front row: G. Dugle, J. Brindley, Hadden, T. Mockford, E. Darlison, D. Simpson.

ARTHUR DEWIS and his family in 1913. Mr Dewis is second from the left at the back. The picture includes Sinkinsons and Pickards. Mr Dewis ran the pawn shop in High Street which was taken over by Spencers and eventually became the library. The picture was taken outside the Mill Cottages (shown at the top of page 63).

MILL COTTAGES, 1911. Originally a mill employing large numbers of Collycroft residents. By the time the photograph was taken the building had been converted to houses.

The Old Silk Mill, Collycroft, Nr. Bedworth.

OLD SILK MILL, 1907. This shows the other side of the mill buildings before they were converted.

COTTAGES AT COLLYCROFT, c.1974. These are original village cottages and show the older narrow line of the road. The turn of the century houses to this side followed a line further back. The other side of them are houses which followed a third line even further from the road.

COTTAGE BY BOTTOM RIVER, c. 1960. Typical of many small cottages in Griff, nearly all of which, like this one, have disappeared.

SECTION FOUR

Chapel Street

TOP OF CHAPEL STREET, late 1950s. Nearly everything has gone: the Hit or Miss, the Double H Meat Co., and the off-licence. There was a huddle of buildings behind them and against the Parsonage and Nurse's House.

CHAPEL STREET, c.1972. The off-licence is on the right of the picture. In the middle is the group of outhouses, originally cottages, built against the Nurse's House on the left.

NURSE'S HOUSE, 1985. The cottages in the last picture really were old, as was revealed when rendering was removed from the end wall during restoration. It uncovered crumbling wooden frames and wattle and daub from the original cottage. The Nurse's House encased much older buildings and its present cellar would have been another cottage.

CHAPEL STREET BEFORE DEMOLITION. The tall well-proportioned building could have made interesting and superior business or professional offices.

CHAPEL STREET. These houses stood where Wyatt's Court has recently been built, opposite Spencer's store.

EZRA CHAPEL, c.1902. Strange though it seems, the building is still there, even though it ceased to be a church at the turn of the century. It was converted into three houses. Ezra was a breakaway group from the Old Meeting. The building is next to Grove Terrace and high in the end wall is a round chapel window. The break from the Old Meeting took place in 1844.

GROVE TERRACE, 1970, with its very distinctive brickwork, by no means an uncommon house-style when built, but now few remain. Most of these are now hidden by rendering.

HOB LANE SCHOOL in the very early years of the century. We do not know any of the names.

HOB LANE INFANTS in 1935. The class certainly seem more relaxed and 'activity centred' than in the last picture.

HOB LANE SCHOOL. This is a typical Bedworth building — unobtrusive, quite pleasant, practical. The windows were a feature and suggest an earlier life in ribbon-weaving. When the school closed it moved to Hazel Grove but kept the name, and the building is used by the Christian Centre.

King Street, Bulkington Road and Rye Piece

KING STREET CORNER, 1919. The gentler pace of life is shown by the groups of men chatting in the middle of the road. Everything on this picture has disappeared. The photographer would have been standing outside the Shoulder Of Mutton pub (now the Nationwide Anglia).

CELEBRATIONS IN KING STREET, 1902. This procession was celebrating the coronation of Edward VII. The shops and houses are adorned with flags and bunting. All the buildings in this picture have gone.

THE BANK, C.1908. As the title implies, there was only one bank at this time, the London City & Midland Bank, which used this imposing timbered building at the top of King Street which looked along High Street. It was not an old building, but was certainly more distinctive than its bland replacement.

KING STREET, c.1903. There are many early views of King Street, almost all taken from this spot. Shops and houses changed with alarming regularity, but there were probably more shops in King Street than any of the other streets, whereas the shopping centre is now moving to the north side of the town.

LIBERAL CLUB, King Street, 1911. A proud building at this time, having been one of the centres from which Billy Johnson had won three general elections. The picture was taken to celebrate the coronation of George V.

KING STREET, 1970, showing the second Liberal Club. The two bay-windowed shops are visible in other earlier views of King Street (pages 76 and 78).

KING STREET, 1974. The King's Head was about to disappear, but further along the street the New Liberal Club was already built, as was the new post office.

BEDWORTH POST OFFICE, 1900. Photograph by Bleasdale of Nuneaton. In the doorway is the bearded Mr Parsons, postmaster for thirty years from 1898. Holding the horse is Jack Draycott; behind him is Bill Froggett. Percy Aucott is in the straw hat and next to Mr Parsons is the young George Jee.

KING STREET, 1925. By now the post office had a bow front. Next door but one is the Liberal Club. On the left is the Old Pheasant Inn and the narrow entrance to Spitalfields, which now leads to the Civic Hall car park.

POST OFFICE, King Street, 1935. This was the new building to replace the one on page 76. It was on the same site as the present office. Probably taken at the official opening, local council representatives are William Johnson jun., Edward Tyler with the chain of office, and clerk to the council Maurice Armson on the right.

AUSTIN & ADAMS, King Street, c.1905. This was the bow window next to the Liberal Club. It shows a jeweller's window full of interest. At the bottom right is a child's inquisitive face, anxious to be included in the photograph.

ADVERTISEMENT FOR AUSTIN THE JEWELLER, 1902. Bedworth was justifiably proud of Billy Johnson, who was not yet an MP but was very popular with the miners. They had built offices in Bulkington Road and a house, Dovedale, attached, for Johnson's use. Mr Austin is advertising a silver brooch with an engraving of the Miners' Offices for half a crown.

SILVER BROOCH, c.1902. This is the half-crown silver brooch sold by Austin's to show the town's pride in Johnson's achievements.

WILLIAM JOHNSON, MP, 1907. Elected in the Liberal landslide of 1906 and re-elected twice in 1910, Johnson had already done enough to achieve national recognition of his work for miners by 1900. Part of the building put up for him and the miners was demolished in 1987 as a result of crass insensitivity by the local authority and studied indifference by mining organisations. It was a sad end for one of Bedworth's few national figures.

DEWIS, CORN DEALER AND BAKER, 1960s. There have been Dewis families in Bedworth for three hundred years. This shop, with large storage space in Croxhall Street, was on the site now occupied by the seven-storey King's House, a reasonable building in the wrong town.

PROCESSION CART. Dewis, like many traders, took pride in participating in the many processions and celebrations. This float is coming out of Croxhall Street. The shop behind was Green's furniture shop, demolished to make way for the 1935 post office.

MOORE'S BAKERY, early 1970s. Dewis's original shop has been extended to the front. This picture was taken as demolition was in progress.

EDWARD ROAD, or the Brickyard, 1950s. This line of tall buildings occupied the space now taken by the post office. The buildings on the right had already gone, to make way for the flats and shops between Edward Road and the Ringway.

= J. FOSTER, =

GENERAL DRAPER,

King Street, Bedworth,

KEEPS A LARGE AND WELL-SELECTED STOCK OF

Black and Coloured Dress Materials.

ALL the year round this Department will receive fresh supplies of New Goods as the Seasons come on. The **Black Dress Department** is always well assorted with the lowest class of Goods both in figured and plain materials, suitable for mourning or ordinary wear.

Crape Cloths,

Cashmeres,

French Merinos,

Habit Cloths,

Wool Poplins.

Serges,

Satin Cloths,

Good Range of

Plain & Figured

Alpacas, &c, &c.

The Drapery Department

IS ALWAYS WELL-ASSORTED WITH HOUSEHOLD LINEN GOODS.

Brown and White Linen.	Toilet Covers.
Damask Table Cloths.	Blankets.
„ Serviettes.	Tapestry and Wadded Quilts.
Coloured Table Covers	Brown and White Twill Sheets.
White and Coloured Counter-panes.	Cotton and Linen Bed Ticks.
	etc., etc.

FIFTY GOOD PATTERNS IN FLANNELETTES.

BEDS, PILLOWS & BOLSTERS MADE TO ORDER.

● ALL THE BEST MAKES IN BROWN AND WHITE CALICOES AND TWILL SHEETINGS. ●

GOODS MARKED LOWEST POSSIBLE PRICE IN PLAIN FIGURES

ADVERTISEMENT FOR J. FOSTER, King Street, 1902. A fascinating glimpse into the materials available at a shop like Foster's. They closed soon after this, possibly due to the arrival of J.C. Smiths who were fiercely competitive.

FIELD'S STATIONERY SHOP, King Street, 1920s. Mr Field married Mr H.R. Lovett's widow, which explains the board above the shop. Lovett originally had a shop and printing works in Leicester Street. He was Bedworth's jobbing printer and his name appears on countless programmes, pamphlets and parish magazines over a forty-year period. He also produced the finest postcards of Bedworth. Most of them were real photographs (the card on the cover of this book is one of Lovett's). Some later cards were machine-printed and sold by Mr Field. They can be seen in the window of the shop.

SOUTH SIDE OF KING STREET, 1920s. On the right is the Shoulder of Mutton. The two shops this side of the Old Pheasant were the last parts of old King Street to go in the 1970s and can be seen opposite.

JIMMY FRENCH'S SHOP, King Street, from the *Echo* collection. This shows Fred Spacey in the door of the shop he ran for Jimmy French. It was opposite the King's Head.

LAST OLD SHOPS IN KING STREET, mid-1970s. Photographed just before demolition. They stood opposite the entrance to the Liberal Club, on the corner of the road to the rear of the Civic Hall. The shop on the left was well known for years as Mittons high-class confectionary and tobacconist, and on the right was Mountford's ice-cream and general store.

CELEBRATING WILLIAM JOHNSON'S ELECTION VICTORY, 1906. The Liberal Club and the Miners' Offices were both in the same road so it was natural that celebrations took place there. The Liberal Club is at the top right of this picture. John Kinder's butcher's shop was later taken over by Mr French.

ELECTION VICTORY CELEBRATIONS, 1906. Not only was there an ox-roast, but special loaves were baked, a band played, and no doubt much beer was drunk. All the men are wearing hats, which explains why there were hat factories in Bedworth, Nuneaton and Atherstone.

CHARLES BOTTERILL in King Street, August 1933. This picture was taken outside Mr Botterill's butcher's shop at 30 King Street (where the King's House office block now is) looking across the street and including the well-remembered Mr Sayer's shoe shop.

ADVERTISEMENT FOR SAYER'S SHOE SHOP, 1902. Residents with long memories remember him sitting working in the window of the shop (page 86) with a mouth full of tacks as he made or mended shoes.

KING STREET SHOPS, 1970. Behind these the land dropped away quickly and there was a basement storey. The modern club on the left is still there, but all these shops came down when Rye Piece Ringway was built.

RYE PIECE, 1970. On the left are the blue brick houses, still there. The large building was formerly Liggins, later Marshalls, who were corn merchants and bakers.

HOUSES IN RYE PIECE, 1970. Two old top shop houses still stand in Rye Piece, next to the park entrance. These cottages and house were to the right of them. Rye Piece Ringway curves through this site.

CATHOLIC CHURCH, RYE PIECE. When this picture was taken in c.1915 the church was surrounded by buildings. It now stands, like the parish church, more clearly apart from other buildings. Next to the church there used to be the police station and house. The church was built in 1883 and the picture was another of H.R. Lovett's fine postcards.

MILD AND PALE ALES.

T. DEWIS & Co.,

Maltsters and Brewers,

KING STREET & RYE PIECE,

——BEDWORTH.

GOOD FAMILY ALE 1s. per gallon.

Supplied in 5, 9, 18 & 36 Gallon Casks.

Agent for Bedworth and District :

Mr. ENOCH RICHARDS, Industry Yard, Mill St., Bedworth.

ADVERTISEMENT FOR BREWERY, 1907. Dewis's variously ran two breweries in Rye Piece, one of which was called Lion Brewery and was based at the side of the present Ex-Servicemen's Club. This building is still in use by the Catholic church.

CATHOLIC CLUB, RYE PIECE, before it became so, in 1970. Originally part of Dewis's brewery.

BEDWORTH STATION, 1905. Originally built in 1850, it would have been a busy station in the days when raw material for the hat factories came by train, and when coal from the local pits went off by train. The station was rebuilt about ten years after this postcard, produced by Mr D.B. Mole, was sold.

BEDWORTH STATION, 1965. This is one of a series of pictures taken by Mr Edmands on the day in 1965 when the last trains ran from Bedworth after Dr Beeching's axe had fallen. The station has been re-opened in 1988.

BEDWORTH STATION SIGN, 1965. These signs are collectors' items and change hands for large sums, perhaps because they have nostalgic appeal for anyone who travelled by train in the 1950s and 1960s.

LOOKING TOWARDS BULKINGTON ROAD FROM THE STATION, 1965. All the buildings were demolished after closure. Bits of platform brickwork remained for the keen-eyed observers. The new station has shorter platforms and a shelter.

BULKINGTON ROAD, 1918. A postcard sold by Mr Field (see page 83). The houses were comparatively new. On the right is the school house for Bulkington Road School and beyond it were the Miners' Offices. At the corner shop on the left lived Jack Wilson, who was a pianist for the BBC and had a musical group called the Versatile Five.

BILLY JOHNSON OUTSIDE THE MINERS' OFFICES. Actually the offices are a few yards behind. It looks as if the man on the right is William Spare, Treasurer of the Warwickshire Miners' Association, and the picture dates from about 1911.

WOOTTON'S HAT FACTORY, Bulkington Road, 1970. This building was originally a factory owned by Paddy Hart, but Wootton & Forge moved here from Leicester Street and eventually the factory was run just by the Wootton family, who lived at Longford. There were other large hosiery factories behind this one. In later years one was occupied by Coventry Hood & Sidescreen, a name redolent of hand-built motor vehicles.

WORKMEN AT WOOTTON'S HAT FACTORY, c.1910. Wootton & Forge had moved to Bedworth in 1887. In 1900 they were employing some 300 hands at the factory here.

SECTION SIX

High Street

HIGH STREET, 1960s. The Shoulder of Mutton stood on the snow-covered corner. The VW car stands about where the manager's desk now is in the Nationwide Anglia Building Society. The church tower is just visible on the left.

HIGH STREET, 1905. On the right are the windows seen on the left of the top picture. The church is at right angles to High Street. The church-like window facing us was part of the girls' department of the Central School which was built on the site of the first Nicholas Chamberlaine Almshouses.

SHOULDER OF MUTTON pub just before demolition. Even in this restricted view two other pubs can be seen. Bedworth used to be a thirsty town.

INTERIOR OF PARISH CHURCH, c.1880. The present church dates from 1890. The picture here is the only one I know of the earlier building, with its small east window and box pews. This was the church Canon F.R. Evans took over in 1876.

THE PRESENT PARISH CHURCH was very much the creation of Frederick Evans, nephew of George Eliot. Since this picture was taken in about 1910 a fine screen has been placed across the chancel.

Rev Canon Evans

CANON F.R. EVANS. One of three or four very influential Anglican clergymen in Bedworth's history, Evans was rector for nearly 52 years. He had enormous influence over the five church schools and over the Almshouses. His only daughter Alison kept a fascinating journal during her days at Bedworth.

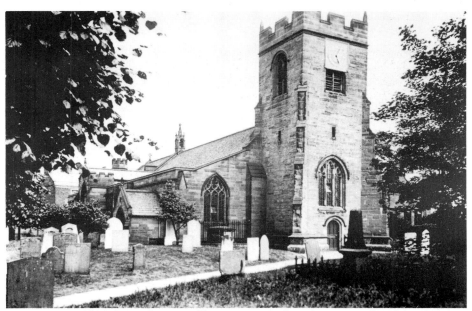

PARISH CHURCH, 1911. A very fine view. The gravestones have been moved and the church is now landscaped into the pleasant surroundings of All Saints Square.

ALL SAINTS ROW. These attractive houses overlooking the church lent a pleasing village atmosphere to this part of the town. The Midland Bank stands on the spot now.

PARISH CHURCH CHOIR, 1948. Back row: A.E. Dewis, B. Shilcock, R. Hollis, B. Rogers, F. Croft, P. Russell, A. Sidwell, G. Knight, B. Stevens, F. Orton, J. Priest, A. Harris, F. Reader, P.J. Bunney. Middle row: M. Deeming, R. Deeming, B. Pratt, Revd E. Dean, Canon Didsbury, J. Crook, K. Whitehead, E. Walker, B. Powell. Front row: N. Priest, R. Dixon, D. Courts, D. Davies, B. Cramp, R. Gardner, W. Whitehead, W. Brown, N. Buckler.

HENRY BUNNEY,

HAIR DRESSER AND PERFUMER,

OPPOSITE THE CHURCH, BEDWORTH,

DEALER IN EVERY DESCRIPTION OF

TOYS AND FANCY GOODS,

Musical Instruments, Writing Desks,

WORK BOXES, COMBS, BRUSHES, JEWELLERY,

GERMAN SILVER & METAL SPOONS, CUTLERY, FISHING TACKLE,

FANCY BASKETS, STATIONERY, ETC.

N.B.—BIRD STUFFER and PRESERVER of ANIMALS, to imitate nature in all its perfection, ON THE MOST REASONABLE TERMS.

ADVERTISEMENT FOR HENRY BUNNEY, who appears to offer an extraordinary range of goods and services from what was presumably a small shop in High Street.

CENTRAL SCHOOL, High Street. Demolished to make way for the Health Centre. The school came right up to the road. Boys and girls were strictly segregated. When it closed, pupils transferred to Canon Maggs School in Derwent Road.

CENTRAL SCHOOL, BOYS' DEPARTMENT. This photograph is thought to date from 1886. The boys are clearly under strict instructions; hair all combed, arms folded, eyes front.

CENTRAL SCHOOL, GIRLS' DEPARTMENT, c.1890. The girls certainly hadn't been told to smile. The front row seem to have unnaturally straight backs. The teacher on the right looks ferocious; one hopes the Bedworth girls had happier days than this picture suggests.

STANDARD ONE, BOYS' CENTRAL SCHOOL, 1910. These boys were all one class: 65 of them. Two years later Mr Jacques, the teacher, committed suicide.

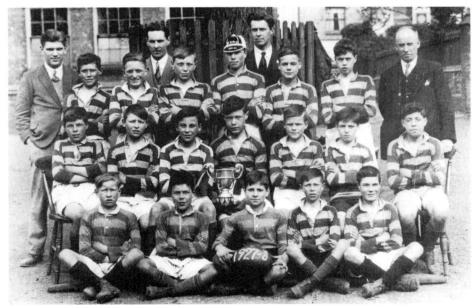

CENTRAL SCHOOL RUGBY TEAM, 1927–8 season. A particularly successful year for this team, which included (middle of back row) English Schoolboy Cap Joe Castle.

COUNCIL OFFICES AND SCHOOL HOUSE, 1950s. The School House was used by the headmaster of the boys' school, which was to the right of this picture. In later years it was used by the Council. Despite fierce opposition from The Bedworth Society and others, the building was demolished in 1987 to provide a site for a new police headquarters.

A H LAWRENCE

AHL BUILT A REPLICA SCHOOL HOUSE HEA THROAD. 1938

PROCESSION IN HIGH STREET. Both pictures on this page were by Ken Bosworth. This one was taken during the celebrations for the coronation of Queen Elizabeth in 1953.

N uneaton Co=operative Society.

❊ *High Street, Bedworth* ❊

EVERY CUSTOMER IS ENTITLED   THE FEES FOR ENTRANCE, and
TO SHARE IN THE PROFITS.   Pass Book and Rules, is only 18.

Grocery & Provisions. **Drapery. Millinery.**
PRIMEST ENGLISH
BEEF and MUTTON.   **BOOTS and SHOES.**

BREAD DELIVERED DAILY

WORKMEN SHOULD JOIN THIS SOCIETY, WHICH IS ESTABLISHED TO DO THE GREATEST GOOD TO THE GREATEST NUMBER.

ADVERTISEMENT FOR CO-OP, 1907. The meat was slaughtered on the site behind the shop, as it was with most butchers at this time. It was then often hung up outside the front of the shop. In the picture below, the Co-op is in the distance, the square building with the canopy outside. It was rebuilt in the late 1920s on the same site.

HIGH STREET, 1913. The Central Schools are on the left. Many residents, or customers of the six public houses on the right-hand side of the street, have come outside to be included in the photograph.

TOWER HOUSE, High Street. The pear tree on the left was at the side of the Co-op, yet the house, so near to the centre of town, had a lovely front garden. The Edmands family lived here. The tower had had a number of uses, latterly for some aspect of ribbon-weaving or hosiery. It looked down over the warren of passages, yards and houses known as Spitalfields, one of the weaving areas in Bedworth in earlier days. Later, the Co-op food hall, now closed, was built on the site of Tower House in the 1960s.

BEDWORTH CARS. Mr Edmands photographed these two on 18 April 1936. They were his first and second cars (a 1929 Morris Cowley and a 1932 Singer Nine). The next day he sold UD 3079. They are parked in what is now the rear entrance to the Civic Hall and the road leads on to King Street.

SPITALFIELDS, 1930s. Looking the other way from the top picture. Big top shop windows indicate ribbon-weaving. The Civic Hall car park is now on this site.

HAUNCH OF VENISON, High Street. A very interesting building, once a posting house and, after the war, included in the first 'List' of good buildings. It was pulled down to make way for the Civic Hall.

HIGH STREET, 1970. In the foreground had been the Central School. On the left is the Beehive, ~~S.DOWN~~ formerly as high as the Haunch of Venison next to it. Then there was a sweet shop and the library. The Civic Hall and Housing Office are on the site now. ~~FISH + CHIPS (CLOUES)~~

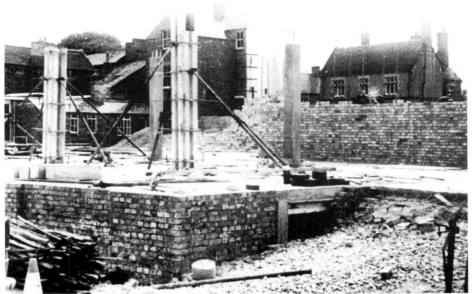

CIVIC HALL UNDER CONSTRUCTION. In the background is the library and the School House.

ALF ENGLAND'S MOTOR-BIKE SHOP. This was a few yards to the right of the old library. It had been a garage for a long time, but there were old top shop windows in the rear of the building. The new library is on the site. A few yards to the right is the White Lion.

DETAIL FROM HIGH STREET, 1913. The Cottage Tavern, kept by Mr Alcott, was the pub serving Ratliffe's Celebrated Stout. Above the window of the shop can be seen the words J. Spencer & Son. The family still run a department store in Bedworth. At this time they sold and repaired shoes. Beyond Spencer's are the Haunch of Venison and the Beehive.

WRONG
SAME
FAMILY)

ATT NOM DER 9 NEWTOWN ROAD 110
NOW NEWSAGENT 1995

COTTAGES IN WHITE LION YARD, 1950s. This was a large yard running along the side of the White Lion pub. The path at the side of the library and CAB follows its line. This line was behind and at right angles to the shops fronting High Street.

SPITALFIELDS, 1950s. Round the corner from the previous picture and part of the mass of cottages, houses and top shops that used to be where the Civic Hall car parks are now. At the far end of this row can be seen the roof of the Catholic church, which helps to pinpoint its position. This was another superb photograph by Ken Bosworth.

A POST BOX WAS FITTED ABACK FOR POOL COODEN 9PM FRIDAY

TOP OF THE TRAMS AND HIGH STREET, 1939. The White Lion is an important landmark for visitors approaching Bedworth from Coventry Road. The tram went to Coventry. Beside the pub can be seen gates with a raised board above them. They opened onto a path to the Zion Baptist Chapel.

ZION BAPTIST CHAPEL. This delightful little chapel was built in 1798. It was extended and altered at times in the last century, but was destroyed in an act of crude civic vandalism to make more spaces in the car park.

COTTAGES BESIDE WHITE LION YARD. This line was beside the path to the Zion Chapel. This view shows the backs, looking towards the White Lion.

COVENTRY RD

WHITE LION COTTAGES. As above, but looking towards Zion Chapel in 1969.

Coventry Road to Exhall Colliery

Mr E. Loach. *July 3*

Dr. to . .

EDWARD RATHBONE,

Wheelwright & General Smith,

WAGGON, VAN, CART & LORRY BUILDER,

2, COVENTRY ROAD, BEDWORTH.

HORSES CAREFULLY SHOD.

WHEELS NEW TYRED AND ALL KINDS OF SMITHS' WORK DONE

Estimates given for Repairing and Painting Waggons, Carts and Traps.

Repairs neatly and expeditiously executed with well seasoned materials, best workmanship, and at ₁

BEFORE MOTOR VEHICLES TOOK OVER THE WORLD, all towns needed blacksmiths and wheel-wrights. Edward Rathbone was one of Bedworth's. This is part of an invoice to Mr Loach, who farmed at High Ash, in School Lane.

RATHBONE'S PREMISES were in the middle of this early picture of the Miners' Welfare Park. Behind the workshops can be seen the roof of the White Lion. On the left was Shortridge's cafe at the 'top of the trams'. Part of the building is now used by the Art Shop.

PARK GATES, C.1930. They remain fine examples of wrought iron and make an imposing entrance to the park.

MINERS' WELFARE PARK, C. 1927. The park was in its early days, as the newly laid-out beds show. In the distance are spoil heaps which covered large parts of this area. Behind them, and along Bulkington Road, can be seen the gasholder. The gasworks were between the Miners' Offices and Woottons hat factory. A new church is rising in its place.

COVENTRY ROAD, c.1910. It is still clearly recognisable, but by 1913 the Baptist Church had been built where the trees are on the left, next to the Downings' house. This section of Coventry Road was a popular spot for courting couples and was known locally as 'The Bunny Run'.

VICTORIA HALL AND CONSERVATIVE CLUB. It had been open about fifteen years when this picture was taken in 1910. The balcony, window and tall pinnacle have been altered, but it is still recognisable as the same building.

MR AND MRS DOWNING IN THEIR CAR, one of the first in Bedworth, and dating from about 1907. The Downings lived in the large house next to the Baptist Church in Coventry Road. The house has been reduced in size and four detached dwellings are now in its former front garden.

CEMETERY LODGE, at the top of Coventry Road. It was kept for generations by the Bosworth family. In the foreground is the war memorial, unveiled in 1921. The Lodge was a fine Victorian building.

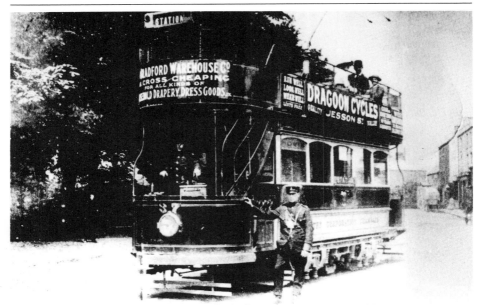

TOP OF THE TRAMS. The tram service ran from Coventry. It opened in 1884 and ran until the start of the last war. This picture shows an early open-topped tram, fine in summer, but draughty down Foleshill Road on a blustery day.

COVENTRY ROAD, 1930s. Again, a tram has just set out and there are even a few vehicles. The White House on the right is a fine building, dating from 1832 and still there.

BILLARD HALL

COVENTRY ROAD, c.1910. All the houses are still there, and still stand well. This was taken just below the junction with Park Road.

COVENTRY ROAD, 1919. Same spot for the photographer, but looking on the other side of the road at this fine line of late nineteenth-century houses.

DR HENRY'S HOUSE in Coventry Road. The superb wrought ironwork disappeared from the front of most houses during the Second World War. Dr Henry had her surgery here before she moved to Black Bank. The house later served as the Rectory for some years and is now a dentist's surgery.

RECTORY LODGE, 1925. This stood at the top of Rectory Drive and the lodge keeper could close the gate across the private drive to the Rectory.

BEDWORTH RECTORY, 1909. It would be interesting to know who the man with the bike is. It could possibly be the photographer himself. The postcard was locally produced yet was rather cheekily captioned 'The Vicarage' by whoever was responsible.

319/6 Main Road, Exhall

IT MUST HAVE BEE
SUNDAY MIDDAY
NOTHING MOVED
EXCEPT ON FOOT
EVENING WAS
THE BUNNY QUIT

MAIN ROAD, EXHALL, C.1930. It was certainly a quiet day. The picture was taken fairly soon after the row of houses was built. They are still there.

CEDARS BEDWORTH

THE CEDARS, Bedworth, 1915. There is a deathly quiet – no vehicles, a few lone pedestrians and Coventry keeping its distance. No wonder that Alison Evans, growing up at the Rectory, regarded herself as a country dweller. Hayes Lane (Idle Lane) was on the right a little way along the road.

DODD'S GARAGE, 1926. A fascinating line-up of early motor-bike enthusiasts setting off on a tour or a race. The Dodd family still sell cycles in the area, but the garage is now a second-hand car dealer's display area.

W. H. DODD,
MOTOR & CYCLE AGENT.
COVENTRY ROAD, EXHALL, Nr. COVENTRY.

SOLE AGENT FOR JAMES AND IVY

ALSO OFFICIAL AGENT FOR

TRIUMPH

RALEIGH, GLOBE, & MOHAWK.

REPAIRS A SPECIALITY.

JIM FREED NEXT DOOR

1 James Cycle   £5 10 0

Coventry Road, Exhall.
'Phone 1 Y, Longford.   192

Received from Mr Loach
the sum of _____ Pounds
Ten   Shillings   Pence
For W. H. DODD,   W. H. DODD
£5:10:0   Motor Agent,
EXHALL, nr COVENTRY
WITH JAMES.

INVOICE FOR A JAMES CYCLE, mid-1920s.
Presumably new for £5 10s., and sold
to Mr Loach from High Ash Farm.

E BINDLEY → ABANDONED AFTER 2 RUNS BOTTOM COVENTRY RD COULD NOT TURN ROUND BEFORE THE TRAMS

DELIVERY VEHICLE, Exhall Colliery. The date is unknown but probably before the First World War. The street is also unknown, but must have been somewhere in the area. It is a superb picture of a vehicle which must have fairly shaken the windows of any houses it passed.

EXHALL COLLIERY, C.1914. Looking across from where Colliery Lane now runs, it shows brick kilns and colliery shaft, but also emphasises how agriculture and mining could live cheek by jowl, for at the side of the tree, within yards of the pit, is a haystack.

Park Road, Roadway and Saunders Avenue

PARK ROAD, 1919. There was considerable development on all the roads out of town between 1895 and 1915, as Bedworth expanded and doubled its population. The house on the left was for many years associated with Mr Bunney.

PARK ROAD, c.1906. The trees look young in this picture, whereas in the one above they appear already to have been trimmed. This shows one of the other fine houses in Park Road, The Limes. Tiny children are watching the photographer all the way back up the road.

SAUNDERS HALL, 1950s. Originally the Hall belonged to the Saunders family who were at their most influential in the seventeenth century. The Club now stands on the site and bears the name.

ARDEN HOUSE on the corner of Saunders Avenue and Tower Road. Mr W.H. Alexander lived here after he left the school house in Collycroft (see page 59) to take over the headship of the new George Street Council School in January 1907. He is seen standing outside the house.

WATER TOWER, 1919. A feature of twentieth-century Bedworth, visible for miles around. The Water Tower brought greatly improved water facilities to the town when it opened in 1900. It is 150 feet high and finally ceased to be used in early 1988. It is a listed building.

CHURCH WALK, 1970. Now a car park. Originally led from the main road from Coventry which, before the Turnpike, ran from Black Bank down the 'Back of the Walls', Saunders Avenue, Roadway, and across Potlidgate Lane to Griff.

HORACE TOPP, tinsmith, and his father before him, worked in these premises and others nearby. His miners' water bottles were known to all local colliers. On Mr Topp's death the workshop contents, including this bench, were removed to Blists Hill Industrial Museum at Ironbridge, where it now functions as part of the living workshop Topp & Mould.

ROADWAY, BEDWORTH.

H. Topp & Sons,

All kinds of Spouting Fixed or Repaired.
Wood, Iron, and Lead Pumps Repaired on the Shortest Notice.

Estimates given for New Pumps, Wood, Iron, or Lead.
All kinds of Miners' Lamps made on the Premises.

RON, ZINC, & TIN PLATE WORKERS,

◆ AUTHORISED ◆

PLUMBERS, GLAZIERS, & GAS FITTERS.

Beer Engines Supplied, Repaired, and Estimates given for same.

ADVERTISEMENT FOR H. TOPP, 1901. Members of the same family were also involved in making organs, some of which are still in use.

METHODIST TEA PARTY. On the left is another Mr Topp who lived in Swindon House, now the Wesley Methodist manse. He used to allow his grounds to be used for church events. This lovely picture shows members in their Sunday best (including a soldier which suggests a First World War date).

THE EDMUNDS FAMILY from Park Road, at a family wedding. In the middle of the back row is Teddy Edmunds. The picture dates from around 1912.

ROADWAY COTTAGES. These pictures of Roadway were taken in the 1950s by Mr E.G. Tooby, who lived in Park Road/Roadway. Both the pictures on this page were taken in the spot where the hypermarket exit now is. This one is looking towards the Coventry Road end of Park Road.

ROADWAY COTTAGES. This picture is looking towards Newtown Road. Many of these cottages were originally lived in by miners. On the left is the building which was Mrs E. Gilbert's bakery until 1939. Mr and Mrs Chard took it over and ran it until 1954. Maisonettes and flats have replaced the whole line. (NEE GILBERT)

RICHARD ∴ ADAMS,

CAB PROPRIETOR,

THE TOWN MEWS, BEDWORTH.

ROAD WAY

Telephone 1Y.

Landaus, Broughams, Stylish Brakes and Waggonettes, Char-a-Bancs, &c.

CARRIAGES & BRAKES FOR WEDDING PARTIES.
CABS MEET ALL TRAINS AT BEDWORTH STATION.

ADVERTISEMENT FOR RICHARD ADAMS, 1907. Known all round the town as 'Crack' Adams, he provided transport for hire from what was called 'The Town Mews'. Later he moved the depot to Leicester Road.

ROADWAY near the junction with Newtown Road. The premises on the left, with the passage along the side, were used by Richard Adams, cab proprietor, as seen in the advertisement above. Haywood's shop was at the corner.

NELLIE BATES OPPOSITE (SWEETS)

Mill Street and George Street

MILL STREET, 1950s. The shops are still there, but the picture is interesting also for the glimpse it provides of the line of houses which once stood behind them, parallel with Mill Street. They were all interlinked with Sleath's Yard. Ashlee (formerly Tesco) stands where the trim hedge is growing.

MRS ALDERTON (CLOTHING) – 1920 –

MILL STREET, 1981. Tesco has moved into Leicester Street and the future of the older property hangs in the balance. It is the last remaining line of eighteenth- and nineteenth-century property of consequence in the town.

HARRY'S BAKERY, C.1960. Housed in one of the oldest buildings, though now much altered and extended.

MILL STREET SWEET SHOP. Joe Clarke, who was born in 1907, was four when this picture was taken of him and his mother standing in the doorway of the shop. Park Drive cigarettes were ten for 2 d. A few years later, Mrs Clarke died and the shop was bought by Mr Bates and is still in the same family.

GILBERTS
SHOP.

BROWNS
Paper
Shop.

THE 'T' ROW IN MILL STREET, c.1960. Similar to Grove Terrace in Chapel Street (see page 69), this line was demolished to provide access to the car park behind Mill Street. The photographer would have stood by the corner door of the present hypermarket to take this picture.

1950/60 - Browns Paper Shop

NEWSAGENT IN MILL STREET, 1931. Brian Stevens is the baby in the arms of his grandmother, outside the shop run by the lady in the doorway, Mrs Gamble. The dog was called 'Shot'.

GENERAL STORE, Mill Street, before the First World War. The shop was run by Mrs Oliver. She is standing with her children, Albert and Lilian. Hanging inside the shop are items of hardware such as buckets and tin baths, and in the window is a wide variety of crockery. The shop now sells fishing tackle.

SHELL OF THE WESLEY METHODIST CHAPEL in Mill Street after the fire which destroyed it in 1941.

TOP SHOPS, south side of Mill Street, c.1960. This line stretched from the Methodist chapel to Church Way. Originally these large nineteenth-century units had some sort of communal power system to drive the looms.

TOP SHOPS, Mill Street. These were purchased to enable the Methodist church to be rebuilt. The large upper windows facing north would have provided good even light for the looms.

GEORGE STREET SCHOOL from the air, c.1945. The allotments and gardens to the right lead into the Sleath's Yard area. Mill Street is on the extreme right. The road at the bottom was once called Industry Yard (the workhouse was there).

STAFF AT GEORGE STREET COUNCIL SCHOOL, September 1907. The school had opened in January. This card was sent by a teacher and shows all her colleagues, with headmaster W.H. Alexander seated in the middle.

CLASS VIII, BEDWORTH COUNCIL MIXED, says the board held by the little girl. It would make it so much easier for us if they had thought to add the year, but they never did. Probably before 1910 to judge by the clothes. The teacher appears on the 1907 group and Mr Alexander is on the right. There are some lovely expressions on the faces of the children.

INFANT CLASS, George Street, c.1912. Miss Ebrey and Miss Watts are the teachers in this delightful class picture. Second from the right, second row back, is Madge Harrison.

LAST DAYS AT GEORGE STREET, 1986. It seems appropriate to include the last days of this school which played a part in the lives of so many residents. In the summer term of 1986 the school mounted exhibitions, interviewed former pupils and endured visits from all and sundry, including me. Mrs Ravenhall is with a class who pause from reading, to be captured for posterity.

FINAL ASSEMBLY AT GEORGE STREET. Headmaster Martin Blows leads the school in singing a specially composed Bedworth song. When the school closed, pupils and staff moved to a new set of buildings called Race Leys, taking its name from medieval field names of the area.

Newtown Road, Woodlands and Newdigate Colliery

NEWTOWN ROAD, 1915. In the twenty years before this picture was taken, all the houses were built, as far as Newtown (where the Queen's Head is). There were open fields beyond until Woodlands was reached.

EXCEPT FOR COTTAGES
LIVED IN BY CLAYTONS
WALES
HEATH RD.   FARNDONS CORNER
                                    WOODLAN DRD
CROFT RD   FROM
                    WOODLAND RD   SLOUGH
                    BROOK   BROOK
                    NEWTONN RD

NEWTOWN ROAD, 1919. This view is looking towards the town. Residents would be delighted to see the road as clear of traffic today.

DETAIL OF PICTURE OPPOSITE. This superb H.R. Lovett card is full of detail. The shop on the left is Swannell the corn dealer. The milk cart has stopped outside Dr McGlashen's house. In the distance is Peake's (by now Franklin's) factory. A man pushes a child in a pushchair on the right.

NORTH SIDE OF NEWTOWN ROAD, 1915. These houses have a sense of unity, with their sturdy wrought-iron railings and their windows unafflicted by double-glazing salesmen.

DR AND MRS McGLASHEN in their new car, outside their house (now two houses – Hilda Villas) in Newtown Road, 1907. The Rector's daughter, Alison Evans, recorded a trip round local villages in this car. The ride was the high point of her week.

76–80 NEWTOWN ROAD, c.1970. These houses pre-dated the turn of the century buildings elsewhere in Newtown Road. Three new houses are in their place.

CAREY FRANKLIN, c.1910. The factory at Newtown (now Toye, Kenning) was originally Peake's, but in 1908 Carey Franklin took over the factory. The woman on the right is Mrs Deeming.

THOMAS

JOHN STREET, off Newtown Road, c.1955. This crowded little community grew up round Peake's factory and was served by the Queen's Head pub, a fine building which still stands.

WARNERS YARD BUTCHER

JOHN STREET, this time viewed from Newtown Road, c. 1955. Counting the chimneys gives some idea of the number of houses, many of them inhabited by large families.

CROFT POOL. It is difficult to think that the large pool which existed behind Newtown Road is now home for some 180 houses and flats. This scene was taken before the Burnside Estate was built and shows the Water Tower in the distance.

WOODLANDS RESIDENTS taking part in what seems to be a Whit Walk, assembling at the Almshouses. Dozens of such photographs exist, but this is particularly good. George Farndon is on the left.

WOODLANDS FLOAT in a field at Woodlands before setting off to join the procession round the town. All the girls have made special costumes.

COTTAGE AT WOODLANDS, 1972. This one stood on the sharp bend where the road turns into Bedworth Lane.   W. ALTON

STAFF AT WOODLANDS SCHOOL, c.1910. They are pictured, with the headmistress seated on the right, outside the school house. The school buildings were demolished to make way for the Bedworth bypass in the late 1960s.

auntie
Win

WOODLANDS SCHOOL PUPILS early in the century. They look a bit more relaxed than some of the contemporary pictures taken in other Bedworth schools.

COTTAGE AT BEDWORTH HEATH. The exact position and date are not clear, but the cottage is obviously the pride and joy of the owners or tenants. Alison Evans visited a run-down cottage on Bedworth Heath in 1908 and found it without glass in the window, and with a mud floor and a hole in the roof.

THE CROSS KEYS, c.1930, when Goodyers End Lane really was a lane and the pub served the residents of Donkey Common.

RELAXING ON A BENCH OUTSIDE THE CROSS KEYS in 1932. From the left: Mrs L. Sparkes (née Marshall), Mr R. Gilbert, Mr J. Ward (with dog), Mr H. Shirley (with daughter Hazel on his knee), Mrs Marshall (landlady), Mr A. Clarke (Cross Keys Sick Club Collector), Mr J. Heritage.

LIGGINS FARM, corner of Smorral Lane. The picture is a bit blurred, but the vehicles are crossing the mineral railway line which took coal from Newdigate Colliery to the canal arm at Black Bank.

NEWDIGATE DISASTER, but not underground. These trucks had travelled along the mineral railway to the canal arm (a barge is visible in the background) and then managed to derail themselves into the canal. Date unknown.

NEWDIGATE COLLIERY, c.1910. One of Bedworth's last pits. Sinking commenced in 1898 and the first coal was produced in 1901. It was nicknamed 'Frankie's'. The two chimneys were replaced by a new one in 1911. It was the last pit in the borough to close, in 1982.

NEWDIGATE MINERS, May 1930. Wooden pit props are in evidence here. The two men with glasses have been inexpertly superimposed by the photographer. One wonders why.

HEV 11
J DENIS

NEWDIGATE MINERS, c.1930. These courageous men seem weary and grimy after a shift at the coal face.

END OF AN ERA. Newdigate a few days before closure. The town had earned part of its living for four hundred years from coal. Fortunately, miners could transfer to other Warwickshire pits.

LAST LUMPS tend to be as numerous as beds slept in by Queen Elizabeth, but this really was one of the last lumps of coal brought out on the last shift in February 1982. It is held by Mr Cox, who spent a lot of his time that last weekend holding up this lump for the benefit of photographers.

ACKNOWLEDGEMENTS

This book has been twenty years in the making. During that time of involvement in local history, especially photographic local history, the greatest pleasure has come from the friendships made and the information exchanged. It is always invidious to single out individuals for particular thanks, but there are twelve to whom I am inordinately grateful. In alphabetical order I start with the *Bedworth Echo*; not for the use of material, because I have deliberately not asked to use their huge collection – after all, they may want to publish it themselves. My thanks go to Alan Robinson and Mort Birch for their work in creating a belief in Bedworth that the past is interesting and that we need to talk about it. Ken Bosworth was a photographer of extraordinary sensitivity. His pictures of buildings have a quality which places them on a very high level indeed, and I am grateful to Ken's widow for permission to use some of them. Geoffrey Bourne, grandson of W.H. Alexander, presented me several years ago with pictures and artefacts about his grandfather, with the comment that he felt I would be able to use them. They are certainly used here.

Jeannie Broadbent speaks lovingly and beautifully in her old age about the Bedworth she knew. She is an inspiration to all who meet her and I have felt honoured to sit and listen to her. Geoff and Ronald Edmands took thousands of photographs over a long period. When they died, Dorothy and her family made sure that a number of local historians had access to the photographs. Consequently, over a dozen pictures in the book have come from the brothers who took pictures for their own interest, but are now informing others. Madge Harrison has been a friend and a fellow enthusiast throughout the years. Always encouraging and helpful, her memories of Bedworth 60 or 70 years ago are marvellous, and her own writing has a literary clarity and style which would grace many a professional writer.

Geoff Hughes and I talk postcards for hours. They are now very expensive and Geoff has been amazingly generous in allowing me to use his collection in this book; sixteen pictures, all gems, are here through his kindness. Dorothy Olner has an encyclopedic knowledge of Bedworth and she has been most generous with her time and her knowledge, in checking facts, helping with pictures and offering encouragement.

When local history is discussed in Bedworth, the name of Fred Phillips soon arises. We all beat a path to Fred's door, and it is usually open and we are made welcome. His collection of material and slides is superb, but the real expertise is in the brain which analyses it all, and here Fred is unchallenged. I am grateful to him for all he has taught me. Arthur and Florrie Stevens are a wonderful couple with an unending fund of memories about Bedworth. They, too, have generously lent pictures for this book. Ted Veasey has fostered an interest in local history in the area which is unsurpassed. For twenty years or more, ordinary people with no historical training have attended Ted's classes and learned to love the subject. I count myself as one of his pupils. Finally, Susan Womersley has kindly loaned me the journals of her mother, Alison Winser (née Evans). Some photographs from them are in the book. I hope to produce an edited version of the journals as a proper tribute to a girl and woman who loved Bedworth.

Many, many others have contributed photographs, artefacts, information or encouragement over the years. Inevitably I have missed some out and for that I apologise, but the following people have certainly contributed to this book and I am grateful to them all:

Mr and Mrs R. Askill • Mrs Eileen Baker • The Bedworth Society • Mrs E. Brown
Mr R. Chapman • Mrs N. Cryer • Mr Tony Davis • Miss Zillah Deeming
the late Mr Ford • Mrs Dorothy Gee • the late Dr Henry
Ironbridge Museum (Blists Hill) • the late Mrs N. Jee • Mr Peter Lee
Mr Jim McMahon • Mr Aubry Mann • Mr H. Nicholls • Mr Charles Norman
Mr Gay Parker • Mr John Priest • Mrs L. Roberts • Mr Alan Shadforth
the late Mrs Emma Sheer • Mr E.G. Tooby • Mr H. Tunniclife • Mr H. West
Mr Bert Wills.

Special thanks to Mrs Maud Johnson for a number of important pictures, and to Frank Wagstaff for the superb picture which appears on the front cover.